The Clever
Camper Cookbook

The Clever Camper Cookbook

Over 50 simple dishes to enjoy in the great outdoors

Megan Winter-Barker and Simon Fielding

DOG 'N' BONE

First published in 2018. This expanded and updated
edition published in 2023 by Dog 'n' Bone Books
An imprint of Ryland Peters & Small Ltd.

20–21 Jockey's Fields 341 E 116th St
London WC1R 4BW New York, NY 10029
www.rylandpeters.com

10 9 8 7 6 5 4 3 2 1

A CIP catalog record for this book is available from
the Library of Congress and the British Library.

ISBN: 978 1 800652 17 0

Printed in China

Editor: Gillian Haslam
Original design concept: Megan Winter-Barker
Additional design: Geoff Borin & Eliana Holder
Illustrator: Kate Sutton

Original photography on location:
John Winter-Barker, Paul Anderson,
Ewan Faichnie, Megan Winter-Barker, Simon Fielding,
Ann Fielding, Richard Fielding, Chris Loxton.

Commissioned food photography by Stephen Conroy,
prop stylist Kim Sullivan & food stylist Tamara Voss
on pages 11 (left & right), 13, 14, 17, 23, 24, 27, 28,
33, 35, 36, 39, 40, 43, 44, 49, 50, 53, 57 (bottom),
60, 65, 75, 76, 79, 80, 83, 89, 90, 97, 102, 105, 107,
109, 111 (left), 113, 115 (top right & bottom left)
121, 122 (top left & center) 125. Additional location
images on pages 30–31 RomiEg/Shutterstock; 32
Kirill/Adobe Stock; 58–59 Jelana M/Adobe Stock;
92–93 Travel Nerd/Adobe Stock; 118–119
Gowtham/Adobe Stock

An original edition of this book was created by Megan
Winter-Barker as part of the University
of Central Lancashire Publishing Course.

uclanpublishing

CONTENTS

Hello! 6

Grocery List 8

Useful Equipment 9

Breakfast 11

Lunch 33

Dinner 47

Sides 99

Something Sweet 111

Index 126

Acknowledgments 128

HELLO!

Just a quick hello from us, Meg and Si, the authors of *The Clever Camper Cookbook*.

We are both keen travelers and big foodies! We love to cook and we believe that even when camping you can cook up tasty and practical meals.

This book began as a twinkle in our eyes on our own exciting campervan adventures. Traveling for two months and never staying in one place for long, we became very good at cooking up interesting dishes full of flavor on our little two-burner stove and finding ways to use up whatever we had left in our tiny fridge. With hardly any storage available in the van, we had to find new ways to cook the meals we loved, without wasting anything!

Since those early days, we have added to our collection of camper meals, taking the van to festivals and traveling the UK with our small daughter.

This book is a compilation of some of our favorite recipes. It is designed to help you maximize space, use up leftovers, and cook delicious, hearty food while traveling in your van or camping with family or friends. We are big believers in real life cooking, so we've worked hard to make sure that every ingredient is used more than once and can be found in most supermarkets. No fuss, just tasty, simple cooking.

The recipes make enough for two people, but they are all really easy to increase if necessary. We have tried to give quantities in amounts you can easily measure, such as cups or handfuls, as we know you're unlikely to have a set of measuring scales in the van, but for most recipes the quantities are really for guidance only and can be adjusted to suit your taste.

We hope you enjoy the recipes, and happy camping!

GROCERY LIST

GET STOCKED UP!

Here is a list of our campervan grocery essentials that we make sure we always have to hand so we can whip up something tasty (plus some useful extras if space in your cupboards or fridge allows).

Old-fashioned/rolled oats

Self-rising (self-raising) flour

All-purpose (plain) flour

Sugar

Bread

Egg or rice noodles

Pasta

Risotto rice

Basmati rice

Can of sweetcorn

Can of baked beans

Can of chopped tomatoes

Rice wine vinegar

White wine vinegar

Balsamic vinegar

Vegetable oil

Sesame oil

Sriracha sauce

Mayonnaise

Wholegrain mustard

Dijon mustard

Chicken or vegetable stock cubes

Tomato paste (purée)

Red Thai curry paste

Sweet chili (chilli) sauce

Soy sauce

Coconut milk

Basil pesto

Curry paste

Ginger paste

Paprika

Mixed herbs

Fajita spice mix

Hot red pepper (chilli) flakes

Onions (red and white)

Peanut butter

Runny honey

Useful extras

Garlic

Zucchini (courgette)

New (baby) potatoes

Sweet potato

Carrot

Red cabbage

Bell peppers

Green beans

Cucumber

Iceberg lettuce

Cherry tomatoes

Scallions (spring onions)

Mushrooms

Mint

Parsley

Basil

Cilantro (coriander)

Bananas

Summer berries

Apples

Lemons

USEFUL EQUIPMENT

Limes
Apple juice
White wine
Pepitas (pumpkin
   seeds)
Nuts of your choice
Shredded (desiccated)
   coconut
Raisins
Condensed milk
Chocolate chips
Corn (golden) syrup
Vanilla extract
Worcestershire sauce
Capers in a jar
Gherkins in a jar
Miso paste
Can of black beans
Chipotle paste
Jalapeños in a jar
Dried yeast sachets

Ground cinnamon
Butter
Eggs
Milk
Crème fraîche
   (or sour cream)
Cream
Cheddar cheese
Boursin (or other soft
   herbed cheese)
Parmesan cheese
Bacon
Sausages
Chicken
Ground (minced) beef
Chorizo
Fish sticks (fingers)
Smoked fish, any
Salmon fillets

We recommend investing in a really good-quality non-stick deep skillet (frying pan), preferably with a lid, that you can use for everything, from cooking fried breakfasts and pancakes, to pasta and one-pot dishes. The better the pan, the easier the dishwashing!

Here's a short list of some other items that we found really useful while we were cooking and traveling:

Regular pan with a lid, for boiling pasta, etc
Flat-pack strainer/colander
   (a great space-saving item)
Silicone spatulas (great for easy washing up)
Garlic mincer (crusher)
Measuring spoons and cups
Measuring pitcher (jug)
Skewers
Two chopping boards
Knives with protective sheaths
Can opener
Bottle opener
Cheese grater
Potato peeler
BBQ tongs
Kettle
Lighter/matches
Kitchen foil

BREAKFAST

GRANNY'S GRANOLA

Although we love cooking in the van, sometimes if you've got a busy itinerary ahead of you a bit of pre-trip prep at home can be a winner. Our favorite thing about making your own granola to take with you is that it's such a versatile recipe that you can mix it up with whatever you already have in the house. Swap out nuts for more seeds, or add chopped dates, apricots, cranberries, dried banana chips, use more honey instead of syrup, or maple syrup... the options are endless!

Ingredients

1½ cups (150g) old-fashioned (rolled) oats

⅓ cup (50g) pepitas (pumpkin seeds)

½ cup (50g) nuts of your choice

Pinch of salt

1 tablespoon vegetable oil

1 tablespoon honey

1 tablespoon corn (golden) syrup

2 tablespoons apple juice

½ teaspoon vanilla extract

2 tablespoons shredded (desiccated) coconut

3 tablespoons raisins

Makes 4-6 servings

Method

Preheat your oven to 325°F/170°C/150°C fan/Gas 3.

Combine the oats, seeds, and nuts in a large mixing bowl. Season with a pinch of salt and mix well. Add all the wet ingredients and mix well so all the dry ingredients are well coated.

Spread the granola evenly on a lined baking sheet and bake in the preheated oven. After 20 minutes sprinkle the coconut and raisins on top and bake for another 5–10 minutes.

Remove from the oven and leave to cool. Once it has completely cooled down, break the granola into chunks and store in an airtight container, ready for whenever you are!

OVERNIGHT OATS 4 WAYS

Overnight oats are a super-easy and healthy way to get a decent breakfast to set you up for the day. Our whole family loves them! You could also make them at home before your van trip and layer them up in jelly (jam) jars, pop the lids on, and take them with you—no fuss, no mess. With all these recipes, it's best to soak your oats in the liquid overnight and then add the other ingredients the next day.

Each recipe makes 2 servings

CHOCOLATE & BANANA OATS

Ingredients

4 tablespoons chocolate chips, plus extra to serve

¾ cup (200ml) milk

1 scant cup (100g) old-fashioned (rolled) oats

2 bananas, sliced

Method

Melt the chocolate chips and mix with the milk. Mix a handful of extra chocolate chips in with the oats if you're feeling extra naughty! Pour the chocolate milk over the oats and leave to soak overnight. The next day, layer with slices of the banana and enjoy!

Tip: You can also use pre-made chocolate milk if easier than making your own.

SEEDED SUMMER BERRY OATS

Ingredients

1 scant cup (100g) old-fashioned (rolled) oats

¾ cup (200ml) apple juice

Summer berries of your choice

1 tablespoon pepitas (pumpkin seeds), toasted

Method

Soak the oats in the apple juice overnight.

The next day, layer with the summer berries (slice the berries if they are large) and then top with the pepitas/pumpkin seeds.

APPLE CRUMBLE OATS

Ingredients

1 scant cup (100g) old-fashioned (rolled) oats

¾ cup (200ml) milk

2 apples

½ teaspoon ground cinnamon

1 teaspoon sugar

1 tablespoon raisins

Method

Soak the oats in the milk overnight.

Peel your apples, core, and chop into small pieces. Add to a pan with the cinnamon, sugar, raisins, and 1 tablespoon water. Cover and simmer over a medium heat for 5–7 minutes, or until the apples are soft.

Layer with your soaked oats once the apples have cooled down and serve.

HONEY NUT OATS

Ingredients

¾ cup (200ml) milk

2 teaspoons runny honey

1 scant cup (100g) old-fashioned (rolled) oats

4 tablespoons of your preferred nuts (we like to use a mixture of peanuts, walnuts, and almonds)

Salt, to taste

Method

Mix the milk and honey together and pour over your oats – it can help to slightly heat up either the milk or the honey before doing this to help them combine. Leave to soak overnight.

Chop or bash the nuts in a Ziplock bag or similar until you have some smaller bits and some chunkier pieces. Toast them in a dry pan over a low heat until they are slightly brown and starting to smell delicious. Remove from the pan and season with a little sprinkle of salt.

Top the overnight oats with the toasted nuts and serve.

MINI EGG MUFFINS

We've added these muffins as a make-ahead recipe as they are
a great healthy snack to have on the road. Easy to eat and no mess,
they will keep in the fridge for 2 days in a sealed container. Perfect
for a roadside picnic.

Ingredients

4 US large (UK medium) eggs

2 tablespoons milk

2–3 mushrooms, finely chopped

5 cherry tomatoes, finely chopped

2 scallions (spring onions), finely chopped

Small handful of finely grated Cheddar cheese

Small handful of fresh flat-leaf parsley, finely chopped

Pinch of paprika

Salt and freshly ground black pepper

Makes 6

Method

Preheat your oven to 400°F/200°C/180°C fan/Gas 6. Put 6 muffin cases into a muffin pan.

In a bowl, whisk together the eggs and the milk.

In a separate bowl, combine the mushrooms, tomatoes, scallions (spring onions), cheese, parsley and paprika and season with salt and pepper.

Tip the egg and milk mixture over the vegetable mixture and mix well. Divide this mixture evenly between the muffin cases.

Bake in the oven for 10–15 minutes until the egg is fully cooked through and not runny. Eat straight away or pack in an airtight container to take with you for a healthy and quick snack or breakfast on the go.

BANANA EGGY BREAD

Most days in the van we get up and go exploring or set off to a new place. But on the odd occasions when we are rained in or having a chilled-out day, this breakfast is the perfect treat. It's no hassle and a bit indulgent—a Sunday morning special in the campervan.

Ingredients

1 banana

1 egg

2 tablespoons milk

Pat of butter

Splash of olive oil, for frying

2 thick slices of bread

Honey or peanut butter, to serve (optional)

Serves 2

Handy hint

If slicing your own bread, make sure they're thick slices. A good farmhouse white loaf is nice, but whatever bread you have will be just as tasty.

Method

In a bowl, mash the banana with a fork. Once mashed, add the egg and milk, then mix together.

Melt the butter in a non-stick skillet (frying pan) and add a splash of oil.

Take a slice of bread and place it into the banana mixture so that it's covered all over and the mixture is soaking into the bread.

Once coated, place the bread flat into your pan and cook over a medium heat for 1½ –2 minutes. Then flip it and cook on the other side for the same time, or until both sides are golden brown. Repeat with the second slice of bread.

Serve straight away with a drizzle of honey or a spoonful of peanut butter, if you like.

If you're going back for round two, just double the banana-egg mixture and then repeat the method, adding a little more butter to your pan when you cook each new batch.

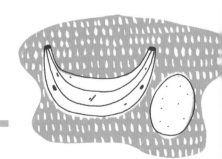

Mix it up

We've made our eggy bread sweet, adding banana and honey, but you could leave out the banana and fry some bacon to serve as an accompaniment. Try drizzling a little honey on your bacon eggy bread, as the combination of saltiness and sweetness is delicious.

If you like a dose of chili heat in the morning to wake up the tastebuds, why not serve with a squirt of tangy hot sauce for a fiery savory breakfast. The amount of hot sauce you use depends on how much you think you can handle.

THE BEST BREAKFAST SANDWICH

Start the day right with a bacon and egg sandwich. Do you like your eggs fried or scrambled? Here's a recipe for both, but Simon's scrambled eggs are the best and are perfect for a large group—less washing up! His secret is "low and slow."

Ingredients

4 slices of bacon

2 teaspoons butter

4 eggs

Splash of milk (if scrambling the eggs)

Salt and freshly ground black pepper

Soft rolls or thick slices of toasted bread

Ketchup or spicy sauce, to serve

Serves 2

Method

Place your slices of bacon on a grill pan with the broiler (grill) set to medium or in a skillet (frying pan) over a medium heat and cook, turning occasionally to cook the bacon evenly.

If you're frying the eggs, add a knob of butter to a skillet (frying pan) and melt over a medium heat so the pan is coated. Crack your eggs into the pan, taking care not to break the yolks, and fry, adjusting the heat if necessary so the undersides of the eggs don't burn. If you like your yolk runny, remove the eggs once the whites have set. Otherwise, cook for a minute or two longer and remove from the pan.

For scrambled eggs, crack all the eggs into a cold pan (preferably non-stick) and add the butter and milk with a bit of salt and lots of black pepper. Start with the pan over a medium heat, then once the pan is warm turn it down to a very gentle heat. Don't whisk the eggs, just stir gently, and continue to cook the eggs slowly over a low heat. Be patient!

Personally we like our scrambled eggs a bit sloppy, but keep cooking until the eggs are nearly at the consistency you want. Take them off the heat, as they will finish cooking from the residual heat in the pan for a few minutes.

Put the bacon and eggs in a soft roll or on toast and serve with ketchup, spicy sauce, or whatever takes your fancy.

CREAMY GARLIC & HERB MUSHROOMS ON TOAST

Sometimes the simple meals are the best. This recipe is so easy but so tasty—a perfect Sunday brunch in the van.

Ingredients

Splash of olive oil, for frying

5–7 mushrooms, thinly sliced

Knob of butter

½ x 3-oz./75-g block Boursin garlic and herb soft cheese (or any other garlic and herb soft cheese)

Handful of fresh flat-leaf parsley, finely chopped

Salt and freshly ground black pepper

Crusty bread, toasted, to serve

Serves 2

Method

In a hot pan, heat a splash of oil and add your mushrooms. Add the butter and stir through once melted. Season with a pinch of salt. Cook for about 5 minutes, stirring occasionally but not too much to make sure you get some good colour on the mushrooms.

Turn the heat down to medium-low and add the soft cheese along with a splash of water. Mix well until you have a lovely creamy sauce. Add the parsley and season with some black pepper. Serve straight away on some toasted crusty bread.

LEFTOVER BREAKFAST POTATO HASH

We love this recipe, it's like a fry up but with way less washing up!
Plus it's a great way to use up any lonely sausages or slices of bacon
that you have left over. If we're feeling like we need some comfort
food, this recipe also works as a great dinner.

Ingredients

4 breakfast sausages of your choice,
cut into chunks

2 slices of bacon, diced

1 tablespoon olive oil, for frying

2 large handfuls of new potatoes,
diced into ¾-inch (2-cm) cubes

½ white onion, finely chopped

2 cloves of garlic, crushed

½ x 14-oz (400-ml) can of baked
beans in tomato sauce (or 1 x 7-oz/
225-g can)

Handful of cherry tomatoes, halved

2 eggs (any size)

Salt and freshly ground black pepper

Serves 2

Method

Fry the sausage chunks in a large, dry, non-stick pan over
medium to high heat for about 10 minutes. When they are almost
cooked, add the bacon and fry everything until cooked through
and the bacon is crispy. Remove the meats from the pan.

Heat the oil in the pan and fry the potatoes on a medium heat.
Keep the pan covered but keep stirring regularly for 10 minutes,
or until the potatoes are cooked. When the potatoes are cooked,
add the onion and cook for another 10 minutes with the lid off,
stirring occasionally.

In a separate pan, put the baked beans on to heat up.

Add the garlic to the onions and potatoes and season with salt
and pepper and mix well. Cook for 2 minutes.

Move potatoes and onions over to one side of the pan and add
the cherry tomatoes to the free side. Cook for a few minutes
until they have softened slightly, then stir through the rest of the
mixture. Return the cooked sausage and bacon to the pan.

Remove half the hash mix from the pan (this is to keep some of it
crispy). Add the beans to the remaining half of the hash and mix
through. Plate your beany hash and then top with the crispy hash
you set aside.

Fry the eggs in the pan to your liking, then top the plates of hash
with them. Serve straight away and enjoy!

ONE-POT MEXICAN BREAKFAST WITH CHORIZO & POACHED EGGS

We both love spicy food, and this is a perfect start to our mornings.
It's a versatile dish that makes for a great dinner as well.

Ingredients

4-inch (10-cm) piece of chorizo, sliced

½ red onion, finely chopped

1 clove of garlic, crushed

½ x 14-oz (400-g) can of chopped tomatoes

1 tablespoon tomato paste (purée)

½ x 14-oz (400-g) can of beans of your choice (or 1 x 7-oz/ 225-g can)

1 tablespoon fajita spice mix

1 teaspoon hot red pepper (chilli) flakes

4 eggs

Salt and freshly ground black pepper

To serve

Crème fraîche (or sour cream)

Fresh chile, sliced

Cilantro (coriander), to garnish (optional)

Grated cheese

Crusty bread or wraps

Serves 2

Method

Put a pan on the heat but don't add any oil. Once hot, add the chorizo and fry until the oil starts to be released. Turn the heat down to medium and add the onion and garlic. Fry for 5 minutes or until the onion is soft.

Add the chopped tomatoes, tomato paste (purée), and the beans (juices and all), then add the spice mix and red pepper (chilli) flakes, and season. Simmer for 5–10 minutes to let the flavors develop.

When you are ready to eat, make four wells in the sauce and crack the eggs straight into them. Cover with a lid and cook for 4–5 minutes, or until the eggs are cooked through.

Serve straight away with a spoonful of crème fraîche and some sliced fresh chile if you like it spicy! We also love to add a handful of fresh cilantro (coriander) and a sprinkle of grated cheese to finish.

You can eat this dish with a slice of good crusty bread, tortilla wraps (see page 62), or even just by itself.

SWEETCORN FRITTERS WITH SRIRACHA HONEY BACON

I think this has to be one of our top campervan brunches. The combination of sweet and spicy bacon, the crispy on the outside and soft on the inside fritters, and a runny fried egg is just perfect.

Ingredients

1 cup self-rising (self-raising) flour

1 US large (UK medium) egg

¾ cup (200 ml) milk

1 teaspoon paprika

1 x 6-oz (165-g) can of corn (sweetcorn), drained

2–3 scallions (spring onions), finely chopped, save some to serve

Handful of chopped cilantro (coriander), same some to serve

4–5 jalapeños from a jar (optional—add to the batter if you like it spicy!)

Roughly 2 tablespoons butter and 2 tablespoons olive oil, for frying

Salt and freshly ground black pepper

For the bacon

2 teaspoons sriracha sauce

2 teaspoons runny honey

4 slices of bacon

Serves 3-4 (makes 8-10)

Method

Sift the flour into a large mixing bowl and make a well in the center. Add the egg into the well. Start whisking the egg slowly into the flour. Then add the milk slowly as you whisk until you have a smooth batter.

Add the paprika and season with salt and pepper. Add the corn, scallions (spring onions), cilantro (coriander), and jalapeños (if using), and mix well.

Heat a non-stick skillet (frying pan) on a medium to high heat, with a mix of 50/50 butter and oil. Once the butter has melted and is hot, add 3 tablespoons of the batter to the pan to form one fritter. Cook until bubbles start to appear in the batter, then flip to cook the other side (roughly 2–3 minutes on each side or until golden brown). Finally, do one last flip and cook for 30 seconds to make sure they are fully cooked through.

To make the bacon, mix equal amounts of the sriracha and honey in a small bowl. Brush or rub onto your bacon. Pan fry or broil (grill) your bacon as you like it, and top with more sauce once cooked.

Serve straight away, garnished with more scallions (spring onions) and cilantro (coriander).

LUNCH

BAHN MI BAGUETTE

This take on a Vietnamese Bahn Mi is one of our favorite recipes in the book. Classic Bahn Mi is served with pork belly, but to save time we use sausage meat instead, which is already packed full of great flavor. The key to this recipe is to buy really good quality sausages which, when mixed with sticky soy and honey and paired with the tang of quick pickled cucumber, pack a flavor punch!

Ingredients

4 pork sausages

1 clove of garlic, crushed

1 teaspoon ginger paste

1 tablespoon soy sauce

2 teaspoons runny honey

For the quick pickled cucumber

3 tablespoons rice wine vinegar

1 teaspoon sugar

1 teaspoon sesame oil

4-inch (10-cm) piece of cucumber, sliced into thin rounds

Method

To make the quick pickled cucumber, just mix the rice vinegar, sugar and sesame oil in a small bowl. Add your cucumber slices and leave to pickle. It will work even if you make them just before you start to cook your sausages, but the longer you leave them, the sharper and more pickled (and more tasty!) they will become.

Heat a non-stick pan on a medium to high heat.

Skin the sausages and take out the meat. The easiest way to do this, is to cut through the skin along the sausage lengthways. It should then pull back easily.

Break the sausage meat into large chunks and add to the pan. As it starts to brown, break the chunks into smaller and smaller pieces so you are left with little sausage nuggets.

Once the sausage meat is browned all over, add the garlic and the ginger paste and cook for 2 minutes. Reduce the heat slightly and add the soy sauce and the honey.

To serve

Baguette (you could use any bread but traditionally this sandwich is served in a crusty white baguette)

Mayonnaise

Handful of fresh cilantro (coriander)

Sriracha sauce, to taste (optional)

Serves 2

Mix well and cook for 5 minutes then remove the sausages from the pan with a slotted spoon.

Spread a layer of mayonnaise onto your baguette and then the pickled cucumbers, as many or as little as you like. Top with the sausage meat, the fresh cilantro (coriander) and if you like it, spice things up with a splash of sriracha sauce.

CHICKEN CAESAR SALAD

This Caesar salad is great as it is so adaptable depending on how much time you have to cook it. If you're organized, you could use the chicken breast from a whole roast chicken cooked before your trip. If you've got time, you can cook the chicken breasts separately. If you're really short on time (and cooking space), buy a rotisserie chicken and use that! At home we would make our own mayonnaise for the sauce, but van life is all about simplicity, so in this recipe a jar of mayo it is!

Ingredients

2 chicken breasts, cooked and cut into strips

½ an iceberg lettuce (or any salad leaves you like)

For the Caesar dressing

2 tablespoons mayonnaise

1 teaspoon wholegrain mustard

1 teaspoon Dijon mustard

2–3 tablespoons finely grated Parmesan, plus generous shavings to serve

1 small clove of garlic, crushed

Squeeze of fresh lemon juice

Salt and freshly ground black pepper

To serve

Croutons (see page 101)

Bacon bits (optional)

Serves 2

Method

To make the dressing, put all the ingredients into a small bowl and mix well. Add about a tablespoon of water (you might need less) a bit at a time until the sauce becomes runny but still coats the back of a spoon. Season to taste with salt and pepper.

Roughly chop the lettuce and add to a large bowl with the cooked chicken breast. Add half of the dressing and toss so that all the chopped lettuce and chicken are coated evenly.

Divide the lettuce between the plates, top with the croutons, bacon bits, if using, and spoon over the extra dressing. Grate some large slivers of Parmesan on the top to finish.

MISO SALMON POKE BOWL

This is a lovely summery and healthy dish that you can whip up in no time with a bit of prep beforehand. We've used ingredients that you'll find elsewhere in the book, but you can try it with all sorts of flavors, such as avocado slices, edamame beans, red bell peppers, or even go really traditional and add some nori (seaweed) sheets.

Ingredients

½ cup (100g) rice

1 teaspoon miso paste

1 teaspoon soy sauce

1 teaspoon sesame oil

1 teaspoon rice wine vinegar, plus ½ teaspoon to season the rice

1 teaspoon sriracha sauce, plus extra to serve

2 fillets of good salmon, skinned and cut into ½-inch (1-cm) dice

For the pickles

3 teaspoons rice wine vinegar

2 teaspoons sesame oil

4-inch (10-cm) piece of cucumber, sliced into thin rounds

Small chunk of red cabbage, thinly sliced

For the sriracha mayonnaise

2 tablespoons sriracha sauce

2 tablespoons mayonnaise

Method

First make the pickles. Mix the rice wine vinegar and sesame oil in a small bowl. Add the cucumber and red cabbage and leave for at least 10 minutes, longer if possible.

To make the sriracha mayonnaise, mix both ingredients together in a small bowl. (We make this all the time, it is good with everything, especially leftover pizza crusts!)

Rinse the rice with cold water until it runs clear, then cook according to packet instructions. Once cooked, drain and leave to cool.

In a large bowl, add the miso paste, soy sauce, sesame oil, rice wine vinegar, and sriracha sauce and mix well.

Traditionally poke bowls are served with the fish raw. If you have good enough quality salmon, add it to the miso mixture in the bowl and coat the salmon well. Leave for 10 minutes, but no longer than 30 minutes. If you'd rather not have raw fish, heat a non-stick pan on a high heat and fry the salmon for 1 minute until cooked on the outside but still lovely and soft and flaky on the inside. Remove from the pan and add to the miso paste mixture and coat well.

To serve

1 carrot, peeled and grated

Fresh cilantro (coriander), chopped

Scallions (spring onions), finely chopped

Serves 2

To build your bowl, add the cooked and cooled rice to the base, season with 1 teaspoon of rice wine vinegar and mix well. Top with the salmon, pickles, and grated carrot, then drizzle with the sriracha mayonnaise. Finish with a sprinkling of cilantro (coriander) and scallions (spring onions).

RAREBIT TOASTIE WITH TOMATO

An upgrade of the humble grilled cheese toastie! We know
everyone has their favorite recipe, but this is ours.

Ingredients

2 cups (180g) finely grated
Cheddar cheese

2 teaspoons wholegrain mustard

2 teaspoons Dijon mustard

2 teaspoons Worcestershire sauce

4 slices of bread

Butter, for buttering the bread

2 eggs (optional)

Handful of small cherry tomatoes,
halved

Sliced gherkins or Caramelized Onions
(see page 108), (optional)

Serves 2

Method

Heat a non-stick skillet (frying pan) on a medium heat.

Mix the cheese, mustards, and Worcestershire sauce together
in a small bowl.

Butter each slice of bread, then make two sandwiches with the
cheese mixture in the middle and the butter on the outside.

Place the toasties in the pan (one at a time if your pan
is small) and cook for 6–8 minutes, turning about every
2 minutes. Squash them down with a spatula and place an
upside-down plate on top to keep them squashed.

Once the cheese has melted and the bread is golden brown on
the outside, remove from the pan and set aside.

Crack your eggs into the pan (if using) and chuck in the cherry
tomatoes. Fry for 4–5 minutes or until the egg is cooked.
Serve straight away, with the egg on top of the toastie and with
tomatoes and gherkins or caramelized onions on the side if
you wish.

THE ULTIMATE FISH STICK SARNIE

A fish stick (finger) sandwich... sometimes it's all that will do.
Minimal cooking but it's a winner. If you want to go veggie, trying
using slices of fried halloumi instead of fish sticks. You could also
swap out the capers and gherkins for jalapeños for a spicy kick.

Ingredients

6 good-quality breaded fish sticks
(fingers)

4 large slices of white bread, ideally
crusty

Iceberg lettuce, shredded

For the tartare sauce

4 tablespoons mayonnaise

2 teaspoons capers

4 gherkins, finely chopped

Small handful of fresh flat-leaf parsley,
finely chopped

Squeeze of fresh lemon juice

Serves 2

Method

For the tartare sauce, put all the ingredients into a small
bowl and mix well. Finish with the squeeze of lemon juice
or a teaspoon of vinegar from the gherkin jar.

Cook your fish sticks (fingers) according to the packet
instructions.

Once cooked, squeeze over a little lemon juice, and build
your sandwich with a generous serving of the tartare sauce
and some crispy iceberg lettuce.

MISO SOUP WITH BOILED EGGS

This recipe can appear complicated at first, but once you have made it a couple of times we guarantee it will be one of your go-to speedy meals. Basically, just chuck everything in a pan and cook for as long as it takes to boil an egg... what could be easier?

Ingredients

3 tablespoons miso paste

1½ teaspoons sesame oil

2 tablespoons soy sauce

2 tablespoons rice wine vinegar

1–2 teaspoons sriracha sauce, or to taste

½ teaspoon ginger paste

4 cups (1 litre) vegetable stock

4 eggs, any size (allow 1 per person)

Egg or rice noodles

Scallions (spring onions), finely chopped

Handful of cilantro (coriander), chopped

10–15 white or brown mushrooms

Pinch of ground white pepper

1 clove of garlic, crushed

Serves 4 for lunch or
2 for dinner

Method

Into a pan on a medium heat add the miso paste, 1 teaspoon of the sesame oil, soy sauce, rice wine vinegar, sriracha, ginger, and stock and mix well.

Rinse the eggs and then add them in their shells to the miso broth. Set a timer for 7–10 minutes depending on how set you like your egg yolk.

After a few minutes, add the noodles into the broth as well and cook according to the packet instructions.

Also add most of the scallions (spring onions) and the cilantro (coriander).

Whilst the noodles and the eggs are cooking, in a separate pan add the mushrooms and remaining ½ teaspoon sesame oil. Cook for 2 minutes on a high heat, season with pepper and add the garlic. Keep moving the mushrooms around and cook for about 5 minutes until they are golden brown. Remove from the heat.

Take the eggs out of the broth and put into a bowl of cold water. Peel the eggs and slice in half. Pour the broth into bowls and divide the noodles between them. Top with the mushrooms, the eggs, and a sprinkling of the remaining scallions (spring onions).

DINNER

PASTA CARBONARA

We cook this a lot in the campervan. It's one of those comforting meals that is super-tasty, filling, and quick after a long day traveling. It's also great for using up leftover cheese or eggs.

Ingredients

3–4 slices of bacon (smoked is good if you like it), cut into small squares

½ onion, finely chopped

1 clove of garlic, crushed

Handful of mushrooms, roughly chopped

1–1½ cups (200g) pasta (spaghetti is traditionally used, but really any shape will do when camping!)

1 teaspoon wholegrain mustard

Freshly ground black pepper

Handful of grated cheese (Parmesan is best, but Cheddar works too)

2 heaped tablespoons crème fraîche (or sour cream)

2 eggs (optional)

Serves 2

Method

Boil the kettle, ready to start cooking your pasta.

Fry the bacon in a hot, non-stick pan. Once the bacon starts to turn crispy and release some fat, add the onion and garlic and stir. Add the mushrooms to the bacon and onions, then turn down the heat to low and cook until the onions and the mushrooms are soft.

In a separate pan, put your pasta on to cook following the packet instructions.

Add the wholegrain mustard and a good seasoning of cracked black pepper to the pan of bacon, onion, and mushrooms. Add the cheese to the bacon mix and stir until melted. It's up to you how much to use, as it depends how cheesy you want your carbonara to be. We love cheese, so a good handful always goes into ours!

Add the crème fraîche to the mix and stir in. Let the sauce cook over a low heat for 5 minutes.

Your pasta shouldn't be far off ready by now. When it's done, drain it and take the sauce off the heat. Add the pasta to the sauce and mix it well.

If using eggs, crack them straight into the carbonara and stir in quickly. This sounds tricky, but it's not! The heat from the pasta and sauce will cook the eggs without scrambling them and you will get a lovely rich and creamy sauce. Serve straight away, sprinkled with black pepper.

SMOKED HADDOCK WITH MINTY POTATOES

We regularly have this healthy dish in the summer, as the mint gives it a lovely freshness. It would also work perfectly cooking the fish on the BBQ for extra flavor. You can substitute asparagus or peas for the zucchini (courgette), if that is what you happen to have to hand, or use a mix of all three vegetables.

Ingredients

2 handfuls of new (baby) potatoes, cut into bite-size pieces

Vegetable oil, for frying

1 zucchini (courgette), cut into ¾-inch (2-cm) dice

2 fillets of smoked haddock, skin-on

Squeeze of fresh lemon juice, to taste

Handful of fresh mint, finely chopped

Salt and freshly ground black pepper

For the dressing

4 tablespoons olive oil

1 teaspoon runny honey

1 teaspoon wholegrain mustard

1 teaspoon Dijon mustard

2 tablespoons white wine vinegar

Serves 2

Method

Boil the potatoes in salted water or 15 minutes or until they are cooked through. Drain and leave to cool.

In a screw-top jar combine all the dressing ingredients, put the lid on and shake well to mix. Set aside.

Using the potato pan, heat 1 tablespoon of oil on a high heat. Add the zucchini (courgette), season with salt and pepper and cook for 5 minutes until it starts to get some color and some almost charred bits.

Meanwhile, heat a splash of oil in a separate hot pan on a medium heat. Put the fish in skin side down and cook with the lid on for 3–4 minutes. Uncover, flip the fish and cook for another 2 minutes. Flip once again, squeeze over some lemon juice and remove from the pan.

Add the cooked potatoes to the zucchini (courgettes) in the pan. Tip over the dressing, add the chopped mint and mix well. Serve straight away with a bed of potatoes and the fish on top.

CREAMY TOMATO & BOURSIN PASTA

The best bit about this recipe is that you only need one pan, which we know is even more of a bonus when you're camping. By cooking the pasta in the stock and tomato, it also takes on loads more flavor...what's not to love? From now on, we might all be cooking our pasta this way!

Ingredients

1 tablespoon olive oil, for frying

1 onion, finely chopped

1lb 2oz (500g) small cherry tomatoes, halved

A splash of white wine

2 cups (150g) any dried pasta shapes, such as penne or fusilli

1⅔ cups (400ml) chicken or vegetable stock

½ x 3-oz. (75-g) block of Boursin garlic and herb soft cheese (or any other herbed cream cheese)

Salt and freshly ground black pepper

Serves 2

Variation

You could also add some smoked salmon, chopped into thin strips, when you add the Boursin cheese.

Method

Heat the oil in a large pan on a medium-low heat. Add the onion to the pan and fry for 5 minutes until it is soft and sweet.

Add half the tomatoes and cook for another 10 minutes with the lid on until the tomatoes are completely soft and can be broken down into a sauce with a spoon.

Add a splash of white wine to the pan and cook for a few minutes to cook off the alcohol (you might need to turn up the heat a little).

Add the stock and the pasta and bring to the boil. Cover again and turn down the heat. Cook for 6 minutes with the lid on, then add the rest of the tomatoes, cover again, and cook for a further 6–9 minutes until the pasta is cooked through.

When the pasta is cooked, add the Boursin cheese and stir in until melted. Serve straight away with a crack of black pepper.

CURRY WITH HOMEMADE NAAN BREAD

We love a curry, but on the road it's not always easy to find a takeout restaurant. The best bit about this recipe are the easy homemade naan. Yep, even in a campervan you can have curry and all the trimmings!

Ingredients

Olive oil, for frying

1 onion, roughly chopped

1 clove of garlic, crushed

2–3 tablespoons curry paste

2 chicken breasts, chopped into chunks (optional)

Handful of vegetables, roughly chopped (cauliflower, bell peppers, and mushrooms are all good in a curry)

½ x 14-oz (400-g) can of chopped tomatoes

½ x 14-oz (400-g) can of coconut milk

Rice, to serve (optional)

For the naan

¼ x 7-g sachet dried yeast

½ teaspoon honey

1½ tablespoons (20g) butter

1 cup (130g) all-purpose (plain) flour

Pinch of salt

1½ tablespoons crème fraîche (or sour cream)

Serves 2

Method for the curry

Remember to start making the naan bread (see opposite) before cooking the curry, as the dough needs time to rise.

To make the curry, add a splash of oil to a non-stick skillet (frying pan) over a medium-high heat. Add the onion to the pan and fry for 5 minutes or until soft. Add the garlic and stir.

Add your chosen curry paste to the pan and cook for a few minutes, stirring regularly. Add just a splash of water and keep cooking until the water has evaporated. You should have a thick, oniony sauce by now.

If using, add the chicken and cook for 3–5 minutes until it is sealed, then add your choice of vegetables and cook for 5 minutes. If you want to go veggie, just leave out the chicken.

Add the half can of chopped tomatoes and half a mug of water. Reduce the heat and simmer for 10–15 minutes, or until the chicken and veg are cooked.

Then add the half can of coconut milk (be sure to shake the can well before you open it as the milk will have separated). Stir through and cook for 5 minutes until hot. Serve with your homemade naan bread, and rice as well if you're really hungry.

Method for the naan

In a bowl, combine the yeast, honey, and ⅓ cup (65ml) warm water, then set aside for 5–10 minutes or until the mixture starts to bubble.

Melt the butter in a pan on a low heat.

Add the flour and a good pinch of salt to another bowl and make a well in the middle. Into the well, pour the melted butter, the crème fraîche, and the yeast mixture.

Start to mix together, gradually bringing in the flour from the sides as you go. It should start to make a soft, sticky dough. Take the dough out of the bowl and knead on a floury surface for about 5 minutes or until the dough is smooth.

Dust the bowl with flour, place the dough back into the bowl, cover with a kitchen towel, and leave somewhere warm for 90 minutes.

Once the dough has doubled in size, knead again briefly to knock out the air, then divide the mixture into three or four small balls. Roll the balls out into naan bread shapes (about ¼inch/5mm thick). As you can see, Si uses a wine bottle as a rolling pin!

We broil (grill) our naan breads for just a few minutes on each side until bubbles start to form in the dough. Keep an eye on them as they burn quickly and you might need to pop the bubbles with a knife to stop them catching,

You can also cook them in a preheated non-stick skillet (frying pan) if you don't have a broiler (grill). Just cook for 5 minutes on each side over a high heat, or until golden brown and cooked through. Eat straight away.

STICKY SALMON & EGG FRIED RICE

On our travels, we used to cook our salmon fillets wrapped in foil on the BBQ, finishing them off straight on the heat to create a sweet sticky coating. We still cook this dish all the time now we're home, just in a pan—either way works equally well.

Ingredients

2 tablespoons sweet chili sauce

3 tablespoons soy sauce

2 salmon fillets

¾–1 cup (175g) basmati rice

Salt

Olive oil

1 onion, finely chopped

3 cloves of garlic, crushed

1 teaspoon ginger paste (optional)

2–3 scallions (spring onions), finely chopped, plus extra for garnish

½ red or yellow bell pepper, cut into thin strips

½ zucchini (courgette), cut into thin strips

Handful of mushrooms, green beans, and/or cherry tomatoes (all optional—use what's to hand. Try strips of carrot or beansprouts for an Asian stir-fry)

1 fresh red chile, deseeded and thinly sliced, plus extra for garnish

2 eggs

Serves 2

Method

In a bowl mix the sweet chili sauce with 2 tablespoons of the soy sauce and then add the salmon fillets. Cover and leave for 10 minutes to marinate while you prepare the veg.

Boil the kettle and cook the rice in a pan following the packet instructions. Season with salt. Don't start cooking your salmon until your rice is cooked and drained. Cover the rice and leave to one side for now.

When you are all prepped and ready to start cooking, put two skillets (frying pans) on the stove to heat and add a splash of oil to both. Once the oil is hot, put the salmon into one pan, skin-side down, and the onion into the other pan. Fry them both for 3–4 minutes.

When the onions are beginning to soften, add the crushed garlic and the ginger, if using.

Add all the veg (except cherry tomatoes, if using) and the chili to the pan with the salmon and fry for another 2–3 minutes. Flip the salmon over, pour over any marinade left in the bowl, and add the cherry tomatoes, if using, to the pan. Fry for another 2–3 minutes.

While the salmon is cooking, add the cooked rice to the pan of onions and garlic to reheat. Add the remaining tablespoon of soy sauce and mix well. Once the rice is piping hot, turn off the heat.

Make a well in the rice so that you can see the base of the pan and crack the eggs into the hole. Fry for about 30 seconds in the residual heat in the pan, then mix the eggs through the rice. Divide the rice onto two plates straight away to stop the eggs from burning.

Flip your salmon one final time to get the skin extra crispy. When the fish is cooked through, place a fillet and half the veg on each plate, add the tomatoes if using, and garnish with the reserved scallions (spring onions) and chile.

The salmon is also really tasty served with noodles or potato salad (see page 103).

WHATEVER'S IN THE FRIDGE RISOTTO

Risotto is perfect for using up odds and ends in the fridge. This recipe makes a basic tasty risotto, allowing you to add your own twist using whatever ingredients are available.

Ingredients

Olive oil

1 onion, finely chopped

1 clove of garlic, crushed

1 cup (175g) risotto rice

2 cups (500ml) chicken or vegetable stock (made with 1 stock cube)

Your choice of cheese, butter, crème fraîche, or sour cream

Salt and freshly ground black pepper

Serves 2

Mix it up

Make fish risotto by cooking a salmon fillet separately, then flake it and add to the risotto when you put in your creamy ingredients.

For Spanish-inspired risotto, add a chicken breast, 4-inch/10-cm piece of chorizo, a bell pepper, and tomato, all chopped.

For a summery dish, add a handful of green veg with some basil pesto, and maybe 1–2 chopped slices of bacon.

Method

Heat a splash of oil in a non-stick pan over a medium-high heat. Add the onion and fry for 2–3 minutes. (If you're using chorizo and bacon, add them now and fry until crispy.)

Next add the crushed garlic. If you're using other meat, such as chicken, add it now and fry until the meat is sealed.

Add any veg that needs a bit of time to cook, such as bell peppers, zucchini (courgettes), leeks, or mushrooms. Fry the veg for 5 minutes, then add the risotto rice. Here you can also add a splash of white or red wine, or a good tablespoon of pesto. Fry for another 2–3 minutes.

Add the stock to the pan and season to taste. Give it a stir and then turn the heat down to a simmer. It should take around 30 minutes for the rice to cook, but keep checking on your risotto, stirring regularly, and add a splash more stock or water if it starts to look dry.

When the rice is very nearly cooked, add any veg that needs a short time to cook, such as cherry tomatoes or peas, and any ingredients to make your risotto creamy. This could be a handful of grated cheese, a tablespoon of crème fraîche, or a splash of cream. Taste and season.

Cook for another 5 minutes until the rice is cooked and then serve.

FAJITAS WITH SALSA & HOMEMADE WRAPS

The perfect dish when you're starving and need food on the table quickly. Here we've gone for a traditional filling, but wraps are a fab way to use up leftovers. Try frying chorizo for extra spice or add cherry tomatoes for sweetness.

Ingredients

Olive oil

2 chicken breasts (optional), cut into thin strips

1 onion, cut into strips

1 clove of garlic, crushed

1 bell pepper, cut into strips

½ zucchini (courgette), cut into strips

1–2 tablespoons fajita spice mix

½ x 14-oz (400-g) can of mixed beans, drained (optional)

Crème fraîche (or sour cream), grated cheese (optional), and scallions (spring onions), to serve

Cilantro (coriander) and fresh red chile, to garnish (optional)

For the wraps

1 scant cup (110g) all-purpose (plain) flour

Pinch of salt

4½ tablespoons (65ml) water

Serves 2

Method

Heat a splash of oil in a non-stick skillet (frying pan) over a medium-high heat. Add the chicken, if using, to the pan. Stir regularly so the meat doesn't catch and cook until sealed.

Once the chicken is sealed, add the onion and the garlic and fry for 5 minutes to soften. Once soft, add the pepper and zucchini (courgette).

Cook for another 5 minutes, then add the fajita spice mix to the pan. Stir so it coats all the chicken and veg. If you're going veggie, you could add half a can of mixed beans at this point to bulk up the dish.

Cook for a few more minutes until the chicken is completely cooked through and the spices have turned sticky and delicious.

Serve on wraps (see opposite) with a good helping of your homemade salsa (see page 64), a dollop of crème fraîche, a sprinkle of sliced scallions (spring onions), sliced chiles, and a few cilantro (coriander) leaves. Finish with a grating of cheese if you're feeling extra hungry.

Wraps

It's super easy to make your own tortilla wraps and you won't have any leftover, but you can always buy a pack of ready-made wraps and use any leftovers with our Mexican breakfast recipe on page 26.

In a bowl, mix the flour with a pinch of salt and the water. Knead for a few minutes until it forms a dough.

Divide the dough into four equal balls, then roll them out on a floury surface until they are nice and thin.

Cook them one by one in a dry non-stick pan for 1 minute on each side, or until you see bubbles starting to form.

Fill them and eat them straight away while they are still nice and soft.

Handy hint

There's no need to take up valuable storage space with a rolling pin. Just dust a wine or beer bottle (or any round bottle) with some flour and start rolling—it works just as well!

For the salsa

5 tomatoes (or 25 cherry ones)

½ red onion

1 tablespoon olive oil

2 tablespoons balsamic vinegar

Salt and freshly ground
black pepper

Cilantro (coriander) and fresh chiles,
chopped (optional)

Method for the salsa

To make a beautiful, fresh, tangy salsa to go with your wraps, finely chop some tomatoes (cherry tomatoes will taste just as good as large ones) and the onion (a red onion if you have it, but a white one will do too).

Put into a small bowl with the olive oil and balsamic vinegar. Season well with salt and pepper and mix together. Keep tasting and adding more oil/ balsamic/salt and pepper until you're happy with the taste.

To liven it up, you could add fresh cilantro (coriander) or even some fresh, finely chopped chiles.

Leftovers?

Any leftover fajita filling can be saved and turned into a delicious pasta dish for the next day. Just reheat the mix in a large pan and add a few heaped tablespoons of crème fraîche. Heat gently until it creates a lovely creamy sauce. Then just add some cooked pasta and sprinkle with grated cheese to serve.

PASTA BOLOGNESE & CHILI CON CARNE

A classic bolognese never fails to please, plus it's fast and easy to turn the leftovers into a chili for the following night.

Ingredients

1lb 2oz (500g) ground (minced) beef

1 onion, finely chopped

1 clove of garlic, crushed

1 bell pepper, finely chopped

Handful of mushrooms, chopped

1 x 14-oz (400-g) can of chopped tomatoes

2 tablespoons tomato paste (purée)

1 tablespoon mixed dried herbs

2 tablespoons balsamic vinegar

Salt and freshly ground black pepper

1½–2 cups (200g) pasta

Grated cheese, to serve

To make into chili

1 x 14-oz (400-g) can of beans (kidney beans or your choice), drained

1–2 tablespoons fajita spice mix

1 teaspoon hot red pepper (chilli) flakes

1 fresh red chile, deseeded and finely chopped

Crème fraîche and grated cheese, to serve

Serves 2

Method

Add the beef to a non-stick pan and fry over a medium-high heat until brown, breaking up the meat into small pieces.

Add the onion and the garlic and fry for a few more minutes, then add the pepper and mushrooms.

Fry for about 5 minutes or until the veg is soft, then add the chopped tomatoes and tomato paste (purée). Add the mixed herbs and balsamic vinegar, season to taste, and stir well.

Turn down the heat to a simmer, and cook for at least 30 minutes with a lid on. The longer you leave it, the tastier it will be! Keep stirring occasionally to stop it from sticking and burning.

While you're waiting, boil the kettle and cook your pasta in a pan of water, following the packet instructions.

When you're ready to eat, serve over pasta with a good handful of grated cheese sprinkled on top.

Chili for the next day

The bolognese recipe should make enough for you to turn the leftovers into a delicious spicy chili for the next day.

All you need to do is heat up the leftover mixture in your non-stick pan. Add one can of beans (kidney beans are traditional, but any can of beans will work) and the fajita spice mix. Add the teaspoon of red pepper (chilli) flakes (or more if you like spice!) and the diced red chile.

Cook for about 10–15 minutes to let all the new flavors develop. Serve on a bed of rice, topped with crème fraîche and a handful of grated cheese. Or it's also great in wraps with salsa (see pages 62–64).

MEATBALLS WITH TOMATO SAUCE (PLUS BURGERS FOR ANOTHER DAY)

Cooking for two can leave you with leftover ingredients, especially if you don't want to eat the same meal every night! With these recipes you can use one packet of meat to create two meals. If there's more than two of you, just use up all the meat for the one recipe and double up on the sauce.

Ingredients for the meatballs & burgers

Olive oil, for frying

1 onion, finely chopped

1lb 2oz (500g) ground (minced) beef

1 clove of garlic, crushed

1 egg

All-purpose (plain) flour (optional)

Salt and freshly ground black pepper

1½–2 cups (200g) pasta, to serve

Handful of grated cheese, to serve

For the tomato sauce

1 clove of garlic, crushed

1 x 14-oz (400-g) can of chopped tomatoes

1 tablespoon tomato paste (purée)

1 tablespoon mixed dried herbs

Splash of balsamic vinegar

1 teaspoon sugar (optional)

Red wine (optional)

Serves 2

Method

Heat a splash of oil in a non-stick pan. When hot, add the onion and fry until soft and translucent. When cooked, turn off the heat and remove half of the onions from the pan, place in a large mixing bowl and allow to cool. Leave the rest in the pan—you'll use these later to make your tomato sauce.

Once the onions in the bowl have cooled, add the beef and garlic. Add the egg to bind the mixture and mix well using your hands. If the mix is too loose, gradually add flour until you're happy with the consistency.

Now choose your flavor! You can cook the mixture as it is (just season well with salt and pepper) or get creative. You'll use half the meat for your meatballs and half for your burgers for another day, so if you want to flavor them differently (see page 73 for ideas), split the mixture in half at this point.

Once mixed, shape the meat. For meatballs, form the mixture into ping-pong sized balls (serve 3–4 per person) and squeeze them gently so they keep their shape. For burgers, gently flatten the mixture into patties to ensure they don't fall apart when you cook them. If possible, put the meatballs/burgers in the fridge for 30–60 minutes to set.

Method for the tomato sauce

With the meatballs, we like to make a traditional tomato sauce and serve with pasta for a satisfyingly hearty meal.

Remember those onions still in the pan? Place them back over a low heat and add the crushed garlic.

Next, add the chopped tomatoes, tomato paste (purée), mixed herbs, a splash of balsamic vinegar, and the sugar (if you have it). If you have any, you can add some leftover grated cheese too—just a little chunk to add some flavor. If, like us, you happen to enjoy a glass of red wine with dinner, add a little splash to your sauce to give it a beautifully rich flavor. Season with salt and pepper to taste.

Turn up the heat and cook for 5 minutes to reduce the sauce slightly, then simmer until you are ready to add the sauce to your meatballs (see overleaf).

Cooking the meatballs

In a separate pan heat a splash of oil.

When hot, add your meatballs from the fridge and seal on all sides, moving them around carefully so they don't break or stick to the pan.

When they're brown all over, add the tomato sauce (see page 71) to the pan with the meatballs to get all the meaty flavor from the pan into your sauce. Add a splash of water if the sauce is a bit thick. Cover and simmer for about 20 minutes. Try not to stir it too much—you have to treat the meatballs gently!

Boil your kettle and cook your pasta in a pan following the packet instructions. Once your pasta is done, the meatballs should be cooked through (cut one in half to check).

Drain the pasta and dish out the meatballs with a generous helping of tomato sauce. Top with grated cheese if you like.

Cooking the burgers

You can either fry your burgers in a skillet (frying pan) or stick them on the BBQ. They'll need to cook for about 10–15 minutes or until they are cooked to your liking. Just keep gently turning them every couple of minutes so they don't catch on one side. Depending on your flavoring, you can serve them the good old-fashioned way in a nice fresh bun and the condiments of your choice, or they also go perfectly with our potato salad for a summer BBQ-style meal (see page 103).

Variations

For more options, here are a few recipe twists you can try.

Spanish meatballs

Add some diced cooked chorizo to your mix and a teaspoon of smoked paprika, then serve with fried cubes of potatoes and a tomato sauce (see recipe on page 71), patatas bravas style.

Mexican burgers

Add 1 teaspoon of fajita spice to your meat before cooking, and serve with fresh tomato salsa (see page 64) and cilantro (coriander).

Italian-style burgers or meatballs

Add some leftover grated cheese to your meat and a splash of balsamic vinegar. Stir in with a tablespoon of tomato paste (purée) and a teaspoon of mixed herbs.

These are just some suggestions, but you can add whatever you fancy to flavor your burgers. In the past we've used pesto, sundried tomatoes, olives—it's a great way to use up odds and ends in the fridge. Just make sure you chop everything really small and combine it well into the mixture. It's best just to get in there and use your hands.

RED THAI CURRY WITH SWEET POTATO

When we've been traveling for a long time, we start to miss some
of our favorite takeouts, so this is a nod to a Friday night in with
a Thai-kout. To cut down on prep you could use a bag of ready
mixed stir-fry veg. You can also turn this recipe into a take on
a Massaman curry by swapping the sweet potato for new potatoes
and adding some peanut butter.

Ingredients

1 tablespoon vegetable oil, for frying

1 red onion, roughly chopped

1 sweet potato, peeled and chopped into bite-sized chunks

1 teaspoon ginger paste

1 clove of garlic, crushed

Large handful of veg of your choice, all chopped into thin strips or slices (see recipe intro)

1–2 tablespoons red Thai curry paste

1 x 14-oz (400-ml) can of coconut milk

½ tablespoon soy sauce

1 tablespoon sweet chili sauce

½ tablespoon sesame oil

Vegetable stock cube

Handful of cherry tomatoes

Fresh cilantro (coriander), to garnish

Cooked rice, to serve

Serves 2 (large portions)

Method

Heat the vegetable oil in a large pan on a medium to high heat. Add the onion and cook for 5 minutes until slightly soft. Then add the sweet potato and fry on a medium heat for 7–10 minutes, stirring occasionally.

Once the onions are soft and the potatoes have some color on them, add the ginger paste and garlic and fry for 2 minutes.

Add the veg (except the cherry tomatoes) and fry for 3–5 minutes, stirring occasionally until the veg is slightly softened.

Turn the heat down slightly and add the curry paste and mix well to coat all the veg. Fry for 2 minutes.

Add the coconut milk and stir until it is mixed well with the paste. Add the crumbled stock cube, soy sauce, chili sauce and sesame oil and stir well.

Cover and simmer for 30–40 minutes, stirring occasionally and adding more water if the curry starts to look dry.

Once the potatoes are cooked, add the cherry tomatoes and cook for 5 minutes until they start to soften. Serve with rice and a sprinkle of chopped cilantro (coriander).

MUSHROOM STROGANOFF

Warming, delicious, and creamy, this is our take on a mushroom stroganoff, using the ingredients we have to hand.

Ingredients

Splash of olive oil, for frying

1 onion, finely chopped

1 clove of garlic, crushed

4½ cups (300g) mushrooms, thinly sliced

Splash of white wine

1 vegetable stock cube

½ tablespoon tomato paste (purée)

½ teaspoon paprika

6–7 tablespoons crème fraîche

½ teaspoon wholegrain mustard

½ teaspoon Dijon mustard

Salt and freshly ground black pepper

Cooked rice, to serve

Serves 2

Method

Heat a splash of oil in a large non-stick pan on a medium heat. Add the onion and gently fry for 7–10 minutes until soft. Add the garlic and cook for 2 minutes.

Add the mushrooms and cook for 10 minutes, or until the mushrooms are lovely and brown and starting to go soft. You might need to turn the heat up slightly.

Add a good splash of white wine, stir, and then cook for a few minutes on a high heat to cook off the alcohol.

Reduce the heat to medium/low and add the crumbled stock cube, tomato paste (purée), and paprika. Mix well and cook for 3–5 minutes.

Add the crème fraîche and both the mustards. You might need to add a splash of water to loosen the sauce a bit. Simmer for 5–10 minutes to let the flavors all come together, adding a little more water if it starts to look dry.

Season well with salt and pepper and serve with rice.

SATAY CHICKEN

This recipe is something a little different to cook while camping. The Thai-style satay sauce is really easy to make and you can make a veggie version by replacing the meat with more vegetables.

Ingredients

2 heaped tablespoons peanut butter

½ x 14-oz (400-g) can of coconut milk

2 tablespoons sweet chili sauce

2 tablespoons soy sauce

Olive oil

½ onion, roughly chopped

2 chicken breasts, cut into large chunks

1 clove of garlic, crushed

1 bell pepper (a variety of colors is nice, but half a pepper per person will do), chopped

1 cup (200g) rice

Salt and freshly ground black pepper

1 fresh chile, chopped, to serve

1 tablespoon freshly chopped cilantro (coriander), to serve

Serves 2

Method

To make the satay sauce, place the peanut butter and coconut milk in a non-stick saucepan over a low heat. Keep stirring the mixture until the peanut butter has melted. Be careful not to burn it! Once melted, add the sweet chili and soy sauces to the mixture, stir, then take off the heat and transfer the sauce to a bowl. Wipe out the pan.

Put your saucepan back on a medium-high heat and add a splash of oil. Add the onion to the pan and cook for 5 minutes until soft. Then add the chicken and the garlic to the onions. Keep stirring so they don't catch and cook over a high heat until the chicken has browned on all sides, then add the chopped pepper.

Boil your kettle and cook the rice according to the packet instructions.

Add the satay sauce you made earlier to the chicken and veg and turn the heat right down. Season to taste. Cook the mixture with a lid on for 10–15 minutes, or until the chicken is cooked all the way through. By the time the rice is cooked, the chicken should be ready.

Drain the rice and season the satay sauce to taste. Serve on a bed of rice (or noodles are good, too) and garnish with fresh chile and cilantro (coriander).

Mix it up

If you like extra spice, add some freshly chopped red chile or hot red pepper (chilli) flakes to the sauce when you add the garlic. You could also add some thinly sliced scallions (spring onions) as a garnish, plus some chopped peanuts or cashew nuts that have been lightly toasted in a dry pan.

FISH STICK TACOS WITH JALAPEÑO & CORN SALSA

We love this recipe for something quick and easy but full of flavor. We like to cheat and use fish sticks (fingers), but you could also cook a fillet of white fish, such as cod, if you prefer.

Ingredients

6 good-quality breadcrumbed fish sticks (fingers)

1 x Mexican Twist Slaw (see page 106) or ready-made (see method)

Iceberg lettuce, shredded, to serve

Crème fraîche or plain (natural) yogurt, to serve

Wraps (storebought or homemade, see page 62), to serve

For the salsa

1 tablespoon jalapeños from a jar, finely chopped

Handful of cherry tomatoes, finely chopped

Small handful of fresh cilantro (coriander), finely chopped

½ x 7-oz (200-g) can of corn (sweetcorn)

1 small red onion, finely chopped

1 teaspoon olive oil

Squeeze of fresh lime (or lemon) juice

Salt and freshly ground black pepper

Serves 2

Method

To make your salsa, put all the ingredients into a small bowl with 1 teaspoon of the liquid from the jalapeño jar, season with salt and pepper, and add a squeeze of lime or lemon juice and mix well.

Cook your fish sticks (fingers) according to the packet instructions.

Build your wraps however you like with the salsa, coleslaw, lettuce, and crème fraîche or yogurt.

We have included a Mexican coleslaw recipe on page 106 that goes really well in these wraps, but another easy hack is to buy some readymade coleslaw and just add the extra ingredients. You could also add hot sauce, extra jalapeños or even the Mexican black beans on page 104.

CHORIZO, CAPER & GHERKIN POTATO HASH

Yes, we also have a breakfast hash recipe, but it really is too easy and delicious not to have a dinner hash recipe too. We kept this one quite simple as the capers and gherkins give it a good punch of flavor.

Ingredients

2 tablespoons olive oil, for frying

2 large handfuls of new potatoes, cut into ⅜-inch (1-cm) cubes

4-inch (10-cm) piece of chorizo, diced

1 onion, finely chopped

½ teaspoon hot red pepper (chilli) flakes (optional)

2 tablespoons capers

2 tablespoons gherkins, finely chopped

2 cloves of garlic, crushed

Salt and freshly ground black pepper

To serve

Small handful of fresh flat-leaf parsley, roughly chopped

1 tablespoon finely grated Parmesan

2 eggs (any size), fried to serve (optional)

Serves 2

Method

Fry your cubed potatoes in a large non-stick pan with the oil on a medium heat. Keep covered but keep stirring regularly for 10 minutes or until the potatoes are cooked.

Take the lid off, turn up the heat and add the chorizo. Don't stir too much as you want to try and get some good crispy edges on the potatoes. Cook for 5 minutes, then add the onion. Cook for a further 10 minutes.

Add the hot red pepper (chilli) flakes (if using), capers, gherkins, and garlic and cook for 2 minutes. Season to taste.

Serve sprinkled with the chopped parsley and grated Parmesan and with a fried egg on top, if liked.

ONE-POT SPICY CHORIZO & BEAN STEW

This rich and spicy dish is perfect on cold nights. It's also great for feeding lots of people—just bulk up on potatoes or butternut squash or even BBQ some sausages and throw them in at the end for a hearty meal. We like it with a good chunk of fresh bread, but you could also serve it with rice (and see overleaf for variations.)

Ingredients

4–5-inch (10–15-cm) piece of chorizo, sliced

½ onion, chopped

1 clove of garlic, crushed

1–2 potatoes or sweet potatoes, or ¼ butternut squash, peeled and cut into small chunks (optional)

1 x 14-oz (400-g) can of chopped tomatoes

2 tablespoons tomato paste (purée)

2 tablespoons balsamic vinegar

1 tablespoon fajita spice mix

1 teaspoon hot red pepper (chilli) flakes (optional)

1 x 14-oz (400-g) can of beans (mixed beans, kidney beans, or whatever you have), undrained

Fresh crusty bread and a good spoonful of crème fraîche (or sour cream), to serve

A few cilantro (coriander) leaves, to garnish

Serves 2

Method

In a large hot pan, fry the chorizo until it starts to release its oil. Add the onion and garlic and stir to make sure they don't catch. If you wish, add potato, sweet potato, or butternut squash to bulk the dish out a bit (if you are short of time, parboil the veg first). Fry the mixture for 3–5 minutes until the onion (and the potato or squash) is turning brown.

Add the chopped tomatoes and tomato paste (purée). Turn the heat down to a simmer. You might need to add some water to loosen the sauce—just half-fill the empty tomato can and that should do it.

Add the balsamic vinegar and the fajita spice mix to the pan. If you like it spicy, you can also add a teaspoon of hot red pepper (chilli) flakes.

Cover and simmer for 40 minutes to bring out all the spices and flavors, or until the potato (if using) is soft and breaks apart on a fork. Keep checking and stirring, adding more water if necessary to stop the mixture catching.

Add the can of beans, juices and all, and season to taste. Turn the heat back up and cook until it is hot. Serve in bowls with chunks of bread and some crème fraîche to cool down those spices, and scatter over a few cilantro (coriander) leaves.

Ways to mix up your bean stew

Bean stews are a mainstay in our campervan because they are so versatile. Often we'll put together an Italian version, which uses celery, carrots, and mushrooms in place of the chorizo and potato. Throw in some mixed herbs during the cooking and you're good to go.

Another easy twist is our take on the French classic, cassoulet. We fry up some bacon and sausages and add them to the tomato, garlic, and bean stew, along with some mixed herbs. We then make chunky breadcrumbs using leftover bread from breakfast to add at the end.

SAUSAGE & APPLE CASSEROLE WITH RED CABBAGE

Van life is not just for summer and sometimes you need a hearty, warming recipe to get you through chilly nights. With the sweet apples and some good-quality sausages, we think that this is one the whole family will love.

Ingredients

4 pork sausages

2 slices of bacon, chopped into small pieces

Splash of vegetable oil, for frying (optional)

1 onion, finely chopped

1 large carrot, peeled and sliced

Large handful of new potatoes, halved

2 cloves of garlic, crushed

1 large apple, cored and quartered

1 cup (240ml) vegetable or chicken stock

2 tablespoons all-purpose (plain) flour

1 cup (240 ml) apple juice

1 teaspoon wholegrain mustard

1 teaspoon Dijon mustard

2 teaspoons Worcestershire sauce

Red Cabbage (see page 108), to serve

Serves 2

Method

Brown the sausages in a large nonstick pan on a high heat. Once nearly browned all over, add the bacon. When the bacon is nice and crispy, remove the meats from the pan and set aside. Turn down the heat and add a splash of oil if you need it.

Add the onion, carrot, and potatoes to the pan. Cover and cook for 10–15 minutes, stirring occasionally.

Remove the lid and add the garlic and the apple and cook for a few minutes. Add a splash of the stock and the flour and mix well to combine.

Add the rest of the stock, the apple juice, the mustards and the Worcestershire sauce. Return the sausages and bacon to the pan and bring to the boil.

Cover, turn down the heat, and cook for 30 minutes until everything is cooked through. If you need to, uncover and turn the heat up for the final 5 minutes to thicken the sauce.

Serve with a portion of red cabbage on the side.

THAI CHICKEN NOODLES

This is another of our favorite recipes. We found that marinating the chicken in coconut milk overnight makes it super tender and juicy once cooked. We love it so much we also cook this at home, marinating a whole chicken in the coconut milk and roasting it in the oven. You can leave out the Thai curry paste from the marinade if you wish and this becomes a take on a delicious buttermilk chicken. We've added 2 tablespoons of the curry paste but alter this to your taste as some pastes are much spicier than others.

Ingredients

1 x 14-oz (400-ml) can of coconut milk

2 tablespoons red Thai curry paste

2 chicken breasts or thighs, chopped into strips ½ inch (1cm) thick

1 tablespoon peanut butter

1 tablespoon sweet chili sauce

Salt and freshly ground black pepper

Rice or egg noodles, to serve

2–3 scallions (spring onions), finely chopped

Handful of fresh cilantro (coriander), finely chopped

Fresh Asian Slaw (see page 107), to serve (optional)

Serves 2

Method

Mix the coconut milk with 1 tablespoon of the curry paste in a large bowl with a pinch of salt. Add the chicken and marinate in the fridge overnight if you can or for at least a few hours.

Once the chicken has had a good chance to soak up all the flavors of the marinade, take it out and cook in a pan on a medium to high heat for 5–10 minutes or until fully cooked and with some good color.

Remove the chicken from the pan. Into the same pan add the marinade and the remaining tablespoon of curry paste. Mix well and on a medium to low heat cook the marinade thoroughly.

Add the peanut butter and the sweet chili sauce to the marinade and mix well. Keep warm on a low heat, stirring regularly. Add a bit more water if it starts to look too dry.

Cook the noodles according to the packet instructions.

Drain the cooked noodles and add to the marinade sauce along with the chicken. Garnish with the scallions (spring onions) and cilantro (coriander) and serve straight away with the Asian Slaw, if liked.

SPICY BALSAMIC PASTA SAUCE

Pasta dishes are great for using up leftovers and creating
tasty, versatile meals. The recipe on this page, and the one overleaf,
are just examples of what we like to cook. Eat them warm or
take them on a picnic as a cold pasta salad. First, This balsamic
sauce is great with pasta, but it's also good served as a sauce for
chicken breasts. Choose whatever vegetables you like to bulk it up
and make changes, such as swapping chorizo for bacon,
or adding sun-dried tomatoes or a handful of
pitted and sliced olives.

Ingredients

1½–2 cups (200g) pasta

2–4-inch (5–10-cm) piece of
chorizo, sliced

½ onion, finely chopped

1 clove of garlic, crushed

Handful of whatever veg you
fancy—such as mushrooms, bell
peppers, cherry tomatoes—roughly
chopped

1 fresh red chile, chopped,
or 1 teaspoon hot red pepper (chilli)
flakes (optional)

3 tablespoons balsamic vinegar

1 x 14-oz (400-g) can of chopped
tomatoes

Salt and freshly ground black pepper

Grated cheese, to serve

Serves 2

Method

Boil your kettle for the pasta, then put the pasta on to cook
according to the packet instructions.

Put a non-stick skillet (frying pan) on a medium-high heat.
Add the sliced chorizo and fry until the oil starts to be
released.

Add the onion to the pan and fry until it is soft. Add the
crushed garlic and the chopped veg, plus the fresh chile or hot
red pepper (chili) flakes, if you like it spicy.

Add the balsamic vinegar to the pan and cook it over a high
heat until it has reduced down by about half.

Add the chopped tomatoes and turn down the heat to a
simmer. Cook for 5 minutes or until the sauce is hot. Season
to taste.

Serve over the drained pasta with some grated cheese
scattered over.

ONE-POT PESTO & POTATO PASTA

This pasta dish is inspired by an Italian classic. We've
used potatoes, green beans, and tomatoes here, but any
summery green veg, such as asparagus, zucchini (courgettes),
or broccoli will work with the pesto. If you prefer not to boil your
vegetables, just cook them separately and add to
the pasta at the end.

Ingredients

1½–2 cups (200g) pasta

Handful of potatoes, cut into
bite-sized chunks

Handful of green beans, or your
choice of summery green veg,
chopped if necessary

1–2 tablespoons basil pesto

Handful of cherry tomatoes, halved

Freshly ground black pepper

Grated cheese

Serves 2

Method

Boil your kettle for the pasta, then put the pasta on to cook
in a large pan, according to the packet instructions. Add the
chopped potatoes to the pan too.

Next, add your chosen vegetables to the pan. How long you
cook the veg will depend on what you've chosen to use. Green
beans, broccoli, and asparagus will all be done in 5 minutes,
so add them 5 minutes before the pasta is ready.

Check the pasta is cooked and the vegetables are tender,
then drain.

Return the pasta and veg to the pan and add the basil pesto
and a handful of halved cherry tomatoes.

Mix well and serve, sprinkled with black pepper and some
grated cheese.

SIDES

SALAD & BBQ STUFF

A cookout is the ultimate camping meal. Here are a few easy recipes to make your lunch or dinner really special and to inspire you to up your outdoor grilling game.

Waste not, want not dressing

This dressing is the ultimate waste not, want not recipe. Once you've used up a pot of pesto, add some olive oil and balsamic vinegar to the jar. Make as much or as little as you want, sticking to the ratio of 3 parts oil to 1 part vinegar.

Put the lid on and give it a good shake to mix in any leftover pesto. Taste and add more oil or vinegar as you like.

You could also add a splash of lemon juice to the jar for a fresh citrus kick. Or add a crushed clove of garlic and a sprinkle of black pepper.

The great thing about this dressing is you can keep it in the fridge for as long as you like without it spilling while you travel around. Just screw the lid back on when you're done and go!

Asian-style corn on the cob

To make the ultimate corn on the cob, try spreading the satay sauce from page 78 on your corn once it has been cooked. Then finish the corn on the BBQ to turn the sauce into a crispy, Asian-style marinade.

Croutons

Making croutons is a great way to add a bit of texture to your salad, at the same time as using up old bread.

Chop your bread into small cubes. Heat a splash of oil in a non-stick pan over a medium-high heat, then add the bread.

Cook for 5–10 minutes or until the bread is golden brown on all sides, then remove from the pan. The croutons will crisp as they cool.

You can keep it simple, or add some flavors to your croutons. Fresh rosemary always goes well, as does a crushed clove of garlic and lots of salt and pepper.

BBQ marinade

This simple marinade will add a twist to your classic BBQ, and it's so easy to make.

All you need to do is mix your leftover curry paste from page 54 with some crème fraîche. You can use a little or a lot of paste, depending on how spicy you like it.

Then just cover your meat with the sauce and leave for an hour or two. Chicken wings or legs work well, and lamb chops or burgers can also be spiced up this way.

When ready to cook your meat, the marinade will turn into a spicy, crispy coating.

POTATO SALAD

Potato salad is the perfect addition to any BBQ, served on the side of burgers or with marinated meats and fish. It also keeps really well in the fridge. The honey gives it a lovely sweetness, while the mustard cuts through with a little tangy kick.

Ingredients

4–5 new potatoes per person (or 1–2 regular potatoes), chopped into bite-sized pieces

1 egg

2 tablespoons crème fraîche (or sour cream)

1 teaspoon honey

1 teaspoon wholegrain mustard

½ red onion or a few scallions (spring onions), diced

Serves 2

Method

Put your potatoes on to boil in a pan of water. After about 15 minutes add the egg to the pan and cook for another 5 minutes.

When the potatoes are cooked, drain the pan. Peel the egg and chop into small chunks.

In a bowl, mix your potatoes and chopped egg with the crème fraîche, honey and wholegrain mustard. Add the red onion or scallions (spring onions) and mix well.

Serve warm or cold.

Mix it up

If you've run out of crème fraîche, you could add a few dollops of mayonnaise or yogurt instead. Some diced gherkins will go very nicely with this variation, too.

MEXICAN BLACK BEANS

These Mexican beans are quick, easy, and super versatile. We like to serve these with baked sweet potato and good blob of crème fraîche or even some crumbled feta cheese, but you could also use them in a wrap with some fried halloumi cheese or layer them up with some jalapeños and grated cheese to make awesome veggie nachos. They would also work really well served with the salsa from the fish stick (finger) tacos on page 64.

Ingredients

1 onion, finely chopped

1 clove of garlic, crushed

1 x 14-oz (400-g) can of black beans (do not drain)

1 teaspoon runny honey

1 teaspoon paprika

1 teaspoon chipotle paste

1 vegetable stock cube

1 tablespoon vegetable or olive oil, for frying

Salt and freshly ground black pepper

A spoonful of crème fraîche or sour cream (optional), to serve

Handful of chopped cilantro (coriander), to serve

Serves 2

Method

Heat the oil in a pan set on a medium heat, add the onion and fry for 7–10 minutes, until soft. Add the garlic and fry for 2 minutes.

Add the black beans along with the liquid from the can. Add the honey, paprika, chipotle paste, and crumbled stock cube and a splash of water. Stir well.

Bring to the boil, then turn the heat down and simmer uncovered for 20–30 minutes. Stir occasionally and add more water if it starts to look dry.

Season to taste and serve warm.

COLESLAW THREE WAYS

Van cooking for us usually means lots of BBQs, but is it even a BBQ without a side of coleslaw? As well as a classic slaw, we've added a couple of twists so that any leftovers can be used with some of the other recipes in the book and won't go to waste.

Each recipe makes 2 servings

REGULAR SLAW

Ingredients

1 large carrot, grated

½ red onion, sliced into half circles

¼ red cabbage, thinly sliced into strips

2 tablespoons mayonnaise

2 tablespoons crème fraîche

Salt and freshly ground black pepper

Method

Combine the carrot, onion, and cabbage in a large bowl and mix well.

Add the mayonnaise and the crème fraîche and stir well. Season to taste.

MEXICAN TWIST SLAW

Ingredients

1 x serving Regular Slaw (see above)

1–2 teaspoons chipotle paste, to taste

3 tablespoons raisins or golden raisins (sultanas)

1 teaspoon freshly squeezed lime or lemon juice

Small handful of cilantro (coriander), roughly chopped

Method

Make the regular slaw using the recipe above. Tip your coleslaw into a mixing bowl. Add all the other ingredients and stir until incorporated.

FRESH ASIAN SLAW

Ingredients

1 large carrot, grated

½ red onion, sliced into half circles

¼ red cabbage, thinly sliced into strips

Handful of fresh cilantro (coriander) finely chopped

½ tablespoon sesame oil

½ tablespoon sriracha sauce

½ tablespoon rice wine vinegar

Method

Combine the carrot, onion, cabbage, and cilantro (coriander) into a large bowl and mix well.

Add the sesame oil, sriracha sauce, and rice wine vinegar and mix again so that all the vegetables are well coated.

CARAMELIZED ONIONS

This is a handy little recipe to have up your sleeve. You can jazz up a BBQ burger, serve as a side with steak, or pop into a grilled cheese toastie, the possibilities are endless!

Ingredients

1 red onion, thinly sliced into half circles

1 tablespoon sugar

1 tablespoon balsamic vinegar

Serves 2

Method

Heat 1 tablespoon oil in a non-stick pan, add the onions and season with salt.

Cook on a low heat for 20 minutes, or until the onions are lovely and soft. Make sure to stir regularly so they don't stick or burn.

Add the sugar and the balsamic vinegar and cook for a further 5 minutes. Remove from the pan and set aside.

RED CABBAGE

Such an easy recipe, this makes a great accompaniment to so many of the main dishes in this book.

Ingredients

2 tablespoons butter

½ red cabbage, finely sliced

1 apple, cored and finely chopped

2 tablespoons sugar

¼ cup (60ml) balsamic vinegar

2 tablespoons raisins

Serves 2

Method

Put the butter, cabbage, and apple into a pan on a medium heat. Once the butter has melted put a lid on and cook for 5 minutes.

Add the sugar, balsamic vinegar, and raisins and cover again. Cook for 35–45 minutes or until the cabbage is soft, stirring regularly.

Something Sweet

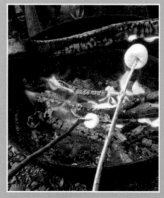

FRUITY SEEDED FLAPJACK

Often our van trips include some hiking as we love to be in the mountains. This flapjack is always in our packed lunch to give us that extra boost of energy to make it to the top! We've used raisins and pepitas (pumpkin seeds) as they are in other recipes in the book, but you could swap them out for other dried fruits or seeds.

Ingredients

1¼ sticks (150g) butter

6 tablespoons (115g) corn (golden) syrup

4½ tablespoons (85g) condensed milk

¾ cup plus 1½ tablespoons (170g) light brown sugar (or whatever sugar you have)

2⅓ cups (220g) old-fashioned (rolled) oats

½ cup (75g) raisins

2 tablespoons pepitas (pumpkin seeds)

Makes 12

Method

Preheat your oven to 400°F/180°C fan/200°C/Gas 6. Line a 10¼ x 8-inch (26 x 20-cm) baking pan with parchment paper.

Put the butter, syrup, condensed milk, and sugar in a pan and place on a medium heat until the butter has melted, the sugar has dissolved, and you have a sweet and sticky mixture.

Add the oats and stir well until the oats are well coated with the mixture. Add the raisins and mix to combine.

Pour (or spoon) the mixture into your prepared baking pan and spread out evenly, making sure the top is flat. Sprinkle over your pepitas (pumpkin seeds).

Bake in the preheated oven for 20–25 minutes.

Allow to cool completely and cut into 12 squares. Pack in an airtight container (you can use parchment paper between layers) and pack to take on your trip.

ROCKY ROAD BARS

No baking, no fuss, these are the perfect campervan treats for picnics or refueling on long walks. Don't worry about measuring ingredients precisely—rough amounts will work just fine!

Ingredients

3½oz (100g) your favorite cookies (biscuits)

5 tablespoons (70g) butter

3½oz (100g) chocolate buttons

2 tablespoons runny honey

3½oz (100g) marshmallows, chopped into small pieces

Serves 2

Mix it up

Try substituting 2 tablespoons of peanut butter for 2 tablespoons of the butter to make your bars extra moreish!

Method

Place your cookies (biscuits) in a sandwich bag or wrap in a clean kitchen towel and bash up into different sizes, from dust to small chunks.

Melt the butter in a pan with the chocolate and the honey over a low heat.

Take the pan off the heat and add the broken cookies and the marshmallows and mix together well. You could also add nuts, dried fruit, or even popcorn to your rocky road bars at this point.

Tip the mixture into a foil-lined baking pan or plastic container—anything that you can put in the fridge. Squash the mixture down so it will stick together when it sets.

Place in the fridge for at least 2 hours. When it has set, cut into squares and tuck in. Enjoy!

MARSHMALLOW & CHOCOLATE BANANAS

You can't have a BBQ without some delicious foil-baked bananas.
They are even better if they come with gooey marshmallows and
melted chocolate!

Ingredients

2 bananas

1 packet of marshmallows

1 packet of chocolate buttons

Serves 2

Method

With the peel still on, slice your bananas open lengthways, leaving 1 inch (2.5cm) or so at each end unsliced. Stuff your bananas with as much chocolate and as many marshmallows as you can! Wrap the stuffed bananas separately in foil and place on the BBQ or the embers of a fire.

Leave the bananas for as long as you can before you give in and eat them. A good 20 minutes will make sure all the chocolate has melted and the marshmallows have become gooey. Unwrap, peel, and enjoy!

S'MORES

This campfire classic is THE way to indulge in delicious toasted
marshmallows. Go on, you know you want to!

Ingredients

1 packet of marshmallows

1 packet of graham crackers (digestive biscuits)

2 bananas (optional)

1 packet of chocolate buttons (optional)

Serves 2

Method

This is such an easy one. Simply toast your marshmallows in the fire until lightly charred and gooey, then sandwich between two graham crackers (digestives) and devour.

You could add some sliced banana or chocolate to your sandwich as well if you're feeling fancy.

COCONUT RICE PUDDING

This is a great vegan or dairy-free option to a classic rice pudding. The coconut milk gives it the same lovely creaminess and using risotto rice works just as well as pudding rice to save on space in the van. You could pop it in some jelly (jam) jars once made and keep in the fridge for up to 3 days for a snack or even breakfast.

Ingredients

Generous ½ cup (100g) risotto or pudding (short-grain) rice

1 x 14-oz (400-ml) can of coconut milk

2 tablespoons sugar

2 tablespoons shredded (desiccated) coconut (optional)

Makes 3-4 servings

Method

Mix all the ingredients in a cold pan until the coconut milk is blended.

Put the pan on a high heat and cook until all the sugar has dissolved, stirring regularly.

Once the mixture has almost come to the boil, turn down the heat and simmer with a lid on for 25 minutes (or until the rice is cooked through). Stir occasionally and add a splash more water if the mixture starts to look dry.

Serve warm or cold, topped with jam, canned or fresh fruits, or whatever takes your fancy!

FRUIT PANCAKES

This basic crêpe recipe is so versatile—you can use it for a sweet treat, topping your thin French-style pancakes with our fruity summer sauce, or for a savory dish add cheese and pieces of fried bacon, or even our chili recipe on page 66.

Ingredients

2 tablespoons butter, plus extra for cooking

1 cup (130g) all-purpose (plain) flour

2 eggs

½ cup (115ml) milk

½ cup (115ml) water

Pinch of salt

Splash of olive oil

For the sauce

1 cup (150g) strawberries, quartered, plus extra to serve

1 cup (150g) blueberries (or any of your favorite fruits), plus extra to serve

2 tablespoons honey

Serves 2

Method

If serving the fruity sauce to top your pancakes, make it first. Add the strawberries and blueberries to a pan with the honey. Stir over a low heat for 5 minutes until you have a syrupy sauce to pour over your pancakes.

To make the batter, melt the butter in a pan over a low heat.

In a bowl whisk together the flour and eggs. Gradually add the milk and water whilst stirring. Then add the melted butter and a pinch of salt.

Heat a small knob of butter with a little splash of oil in a non-stick pan. Then, on a medium-high heat, add a good spoonful of your pancake batter.

Tilt the pan around so that the batter covers the whole pan in a thin layer. Cook until the pancake is turning golden (usually 1–2 minutes on each side), flipping it halfway, or tossing if you're brave!

Serve straight away, with the sauce poured over and dotted with the extra fruit. This quantity of batter will make about 6–8 pancakes.

MISO CARAMEL BANOFFEE PIES

This recipe is a perfect dessert for a special occasion celebrated in the van. The miso gives the caramel a lovely savory and salty taste that goes so well with the sweet base and cream. We use a no-bake method so you could make it in the van or you could prep at home and bring with you. We use glass jars with screw-top lids to layer our pie instead of a tart case for easy transporting!

Ingredients

3–4 Hob Nob biscuits (or your favorite rolled oat or oatmeal cookie), you need about 2oz (55g)

2 tablespoons (25g) butter, melted

For the caramel

3 tablespoons (40g) butter

3¼ tablespoons (40g) sugar

½ tablespoon miso paste

¼ x 14-oz (400-g) can condensed milk (about 5 tablespoons)

For the topping

1–2 ripe bananas

A little whipped cream (whip your own, or use aerated squirty cream in a can)

2 tablespoons chocolate chips

Serves 2

Method

Smash the cookies in a bowl until they are fine crumbs. Add the melted butter and mix well. Divide between the jars and press into the bottom so to make a firm and smooth base. Chill in the fridge for 10 minutes.

While the base is chilling, make the caramel. Melt the butter and sugar in a non-stick pan on a low heat, stirring continuously. Then add the miso paste and mix well. Add the condensed milk and bring to the boil for 1 minute, then remove from the heat and pour over the chilled bases. Chill in the fridge for 1 hour, or until set.

Once set, slice the bananas and layer onto the caramel. Top with the whipped cream and the chocolate chips and dig in! (Food safety note: If making in advance, do not add the cream until just before serving, and keep it chilled until use.)

INDEX

A

apples: apple crumble oats 16
   red cabbage 108
   sausage & apple casserole 88
Asian slaw 107
Asian-style corn on the cob 100

B

bacon: the best breakfast sandwich
   21
   leftover breakfast potato hash 25
   pasta carbonara 48
   sausage & apple casserole 88
   sriracha honey bacon 29
bahn mi baguette 34–5
baked beans: leftover breakfast
   potato hash 25
balsamic pasta sauce 94
bananas: banana eggy bread 18–19
   chocolate & banana oats 15
   marshmallow & chocolate bananas
   117
   miso caramel banoffee pies 124
banoffee pies, miso caramel 124
barbecues 100
BBQ marinade 101
beans: chili con carne 66–7
   fajitas with salsa & homemade
   wraps 62–4
   one-pot Mexican breakfast 26
   one-pot spicy chorizo & bean stew
   85–6
beef: burgers 70, 72–3
   chili con carne 66–7
   meatballs with tomato sauce 70–3
   pasta bolognese 66–7
berries: seeded summer berry oats
   15
biscuits *see* cookies

black beans, Mexican 104
bolognese sauce 66–7
Boursin : creamy garlic & herb
   mushrooms on toast 22
   creamy tomato & Boursin pasta 52
bread: bahn mi baguette 34–5
   banana eggy bread 18–19
   croutons 101
   homemade naan bread 54–5
   see also sandwiches; toast
burgers 70, 72–3

C

Caesar dressing 37
capers: chorizo, caper & gherkin
   potato hash 82
   tartare sauce 42
caramel: miso caramel banoffee
   pies 124
caramelized onions 108
carrots: coleslaw 106–7
cheese: creamy garlic & herb
   mushrooms on toast 22
   creamy tomato & Boursin pasta 52
   pasta carbonara 48
   rarebit toastie with tomato 41
chicken: chicken Caesar salad 37
   curry with homemade naan bread
   54
   fajitas with salsa & homemade
   wraps 62–4
   satay chicken 78–9
   Spanish-inspired risotto 61
   Thai chicken noodles 91
chili con carne 66–7
chocolate: marshmallow & chocolate
   bananas 117
   rocky road bars 114
   s'mores 117

chorizo: chorizo, caper & gherkin
   potato hash 82
   one-pot Mexican breakfast 26
   one-pot spicy chorizo & bean stew
   85–6
   Spanish-inspired risotto 61
   Spanish meatballs 73
   spicy balsamic pasta sauce 94
coconut rice pudding 120
coleslaw three ways 106–7
cookies (biscuits): miso caramel
   banoffee pies 124
   rocky road bars 114
   s'mores 117
corn (sweetcorn): Asian-style corn
   on the cob 100
   jalapeno & corn salsa 81
   sweetcorn fritters 29
croutons 101
cucumber: pickles 34–5, 38–9
curry: BBQ marinade 101
   curry with homemade naan bread
   54
   red Thai curry with sweet potato 74
   Thai chicken noodles 91

D

dressing: waste not, want not 100

E

eggs: banana eggy bread 18–19
   the best breakfast sandwich 21
   miso soup with boiled eggs 45
   one-pot Mexican breakfast 26
   pasta carbonara 48
   sticky salmon & egg fried rice
   56–7
equipment 9

F
fajitas with salsa & homemade wraps
    62-4
fish fingers: fish finger tacos 81
    the ultimate fish finger sarnie 42
flapjack 112
fritters, sweetcorn 29
fruit pancakes 123

G
gherkins: chorizo, caper & gherkin
    potato hash 82
    tartare sauce 42
granola, Granny's 12

H
honey nut oats 16

I
ingredients 8-9
Italian-style burgers or meatballs 73

J
jalapeno & corn salsa 81

L
leftover breakfast potato hash 25
leftover pasta dishes 94-6

M
marinade, BBQ 101
marshmallows: marshmallow &
    chocolate bananas 117
    rocky road bars 114
    s'mores 117
mayonnaise: coleslaw 106
    sriracha mayonnaise 38-9
    tartare sauce 42
meatballs with tomato sauce 70-3
Mexican black beans 104
Mexican burgers 73
Mexican twist slaw 106
miso caramel banoffee pies 124
miso salmon poke bowl 38-9
miso soup with boiled eggs 45

muffins, mini egg 17
mushrooms: creamy garlic & herb
    mushrooms on toast 22
    mini egg muffins 17
    mushroom stroganoff 77
    pasta bolognese 66-7
    pasta carbonara 48

N
naan bread 54-5
noodles, Thai chicken 91
nuts: Granny's granola 12

O
oats: apple crumble oats 16
    chocolate & banana oats 15
    fruity, seeded flapjack 112
    Granny's granola 12
    honey nut oats 16
    seeded summer berry oats 15
one-pot Mexican breakfast 26
one-pot pesto & potato pasta 96
one-pot spicy chorizo & bean stew
    85-6
onions, caramelized 108

P
pancakes, fruit 123
pasta: creamy tomato & Boursin
    pasta 52
    leftover pasta dishes 94-6
    meatballs with tomato sauce 70-3
    one-pot pesto & potato pasta 96
    pasta bolognese 66-7
    pasta carbonara 48
    spicy balsamic pasta sauce 94
peanut butter: satay chicken 78-9
peppers (bell): fajitas with salsa &
    homemade wraps 62-4
    satay chicken 78-9
    Spanish-inspired risotto 61
pesto: one-pot pesto & potato pasta
    96
    waste not, want not dressing 100

pickles 38-9
    quick pickled cucumber 34-5
poke bowl, miso salmon 38-9
potatoes: chorizo, caper & gherkin
    potato hash 82
    leftover breakfast potato hash 25
    one-pot pesto & potato pasta 96
    one-pot spicy chorizo & bean stew
        85-6
    potato salad 103
    sausage & apple casserole 88
    smoked haddock with minty
        potatoes 51
pumpkin seeds: fruity, seeded
    flapjack 112
    Granny's granola 12
    seeded summer berry oats 15

R
raisins: fruity, seeded flapjack 112
rarebit toastie with tomato 41
red cabbage 108
    coleslaw 106-7
    pickles 38-9
    sausage & apple casserole 88
red Thai curry with sweet potato 74
rice: coconut rice pudding 120
    satay chicken 78-9
    sticky salmon & egg fried rice
        56-7
    whatever's in the fridge risotto 61
rocky road bars 114

S
salads 100
    chicken Caesar salad 37
    potato salad 103
salmon: fish risotto 61
    miso salmon poke bowl 38-9
    sticky salmon & egg fried rice
        56-7
salsa 64
    jalapeno & corn salsa 81
sandwiches: the best breakfast
    sandwich 21

the ultimate fish finger sarnie 42
satay chicken 78–9
sausages: bahn mi baguette 34–5
  leftover breakfast potato hash 25
  sausage & apple casserole 88
  see also chorizo
smoked haddock with minty potatoes
  51
s'mores 117
soup, miso 45
Spanish meatballs 73
sriracha honey bacon 29
sriracha mayonnaise 38–9
stews: one-pot spicy chorizo & bean
  stew 85–6
  sausage & apple casserole 88
strawberries: fruit pancakes 123
stroganoff, mushroom 77
sweet potato, red Thai curry with 74
sweetcorn see corn

T
tacos, fish finger 81
tartare sauce 42
Thai chicken noodles 91
toast: creamy garlic & herb
    mushrooms on toast 22
  rarebit toastie with tomato 41
tomatoes: creamy tomato & Boursin
    pasta 52
  jalapeno & corn salsa 81
  meatballs with tomato sauce 70–3
  mini egg muffins 17
  one-pot Mexican breakfast 26
  one-pot spicy chorizo & bean stew
    85–6
  pasta bolognese 66–7
  rarebit toastie with tomato 41
  salsa 64
  spicy balsamic pasta sauce 94
tortilla wraps 62–3

U
the ultimate fish finger sarnie 42

V
vegetables: curry with homemade
    naan bread 54
  red Thai curry 74
  spicy balsamic pasta sauce 94

W
waste not, want not dressing 100
whatever's in the fridge risotto 61
wraps 62–3

ACKNOWLEDGMENTS

I've only been able to create this book with a massive amount of support and help from friends and family. It really has been a huge collaborative effort, and I've been lucky to work with so many talented people. So... to everyone who helped taste recipes, to the Andersons, especially Paul, and to everyone who came on early morning, freezing cold photoshoots, especially Ewan. To all of the Fieldings, especially Ann and Dave for letting me use Dolly the van and their house for photoshoots. To Sally, John, and Sam for their continuing belief and support, and lastly to Si, my co-author and traveling buddy, for the massive amounts of help and support you have given me throughout the project—this book would not have been possible without you.

Thank you!
Meg